C000269087

A Coruña

Lighthouse of the Atlantic

susaeta

From the northern balcony of the Tower of Hercules one can get a superb view of the Atlantic Ocean and the outline of the coast between Orzán and Herminia Points.

Edited by:
Thema, Equipo Editorial, S.A.

Photography by:
Frederic Camallonga

Translated by:
Carole Patton

For the corresponding subjects:
© Museo Arqueológico –
Ayuntamiento de A Coruña
© Museo de Belas Artes da Coruña

© SUSAETA EDICIONES S.A.
Campezo, s/n – 28022 Madrid (Spain)
Telephone: 913 009 100
Fax: 913 009 118

The multicoloured products of the sea, proudly displayed here as if they were a family portrait, are essential ingredients of the succulent cuisine of A Coruña.

Contents

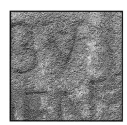

The so-called "city of glass" defines the beauty of an eminently seaboard town whose main activity is fishing.

A Coruña

Lighthouse of the Atlantic

Ouh, meiga cibdá da Cruña,
cibdá que por sobre os mares
érgues a cabeza altiva,
cal onte nas túas murallas
o brazo de María Pita.

(Oh, my bewitching city of A Coruña,
City that raises its head
Proudly over the seas,
Like yesteryear in your walls
The arm of María Pita)
Curros Enríquez

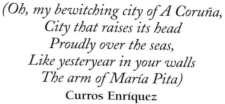

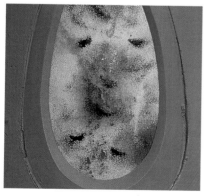

Fun
In the historical *Calle Real* we can see how the inhabitants of this city enjoy themselves in the evening.

Imagination
A detail on a streetlamp allows one to imagine faces.

Light
Resting in the sunshine, surrounded by shaded arcades whose darkness seems to enhance the strong light.

Uneasiness
Charon, the ferryman of the Styx, looks to where souls are lost.

Balance
A ride on the bike leads one to thinking that time rolls on without any haste whatsoever.

Rationality
The tram, as a means of public transport, helps to keep the city air clean.

Spectacular panoramic view over Orzán Bay seen from the top of the Tower of Hercules.

A Coruña

Lighthouse of the Atlantic

THE CITY AT THE END OF THE WORLD

The Mark of Hercules

The origin of A Coruña and its famous tower are related with the famous Twelve Labours of the legendary Hercules or Heracles, as he was called by the Romans. These Labours were ritual feats that the hero had to accomplish in order to pay for a crime carried out in a fit of rage. The tenth of these Labours consisted in stealing the marvellous red oxen of Geryon, a three-bodied giant joined by the waist that ruled in the extreme West. After gathering an army with people from Crete, Heracles headed for the west, and when he reached the end of the Mediterranean Sea, built two huge columns and opened

Parque de Santa Margarita

Strolling along the smooth, winding paths of this peaceful park, people out for a walk are carried away by their dreams.

View to the South

Far beyond the dark ceiling of clouds, the inlet opens up to the sea like an impossible journey whilst one gazes into the horizon, reminiscing about the legendary origin of A Coruña and its surroundings.

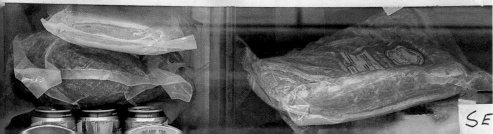

The Pantry of Galicia

A display of all kinds of locally cured meats such as *cecina*, *chorizo* sausages or cracklings and *tetilla* cheeses certainly whet the appetite.

a channel joining them to the Ocean. As the oxen of Geryon were guarded by the shepherd, Eurytrion, son of Ares, and by Orthrus, a two-headed dog, Hercules slew them both and later fought with King Geryon, whom he also killed. In order to prove what he had achieved, Hercules cut off the king's head and buried it at a place near the coast, over which he erected a tower, and beside which he founded a city. This is the mythical origin of the Tower of Hercules and the city of A Coruña.

The historical origin of the city is equally dramatic. It is said that the oldest settlements here are related to primitive Iberian and Celtic tribes, whose dolmens, menhirs and *castros* re-

Modernism
Modernist-style architecture was adopted by the bourgeoisie of A Coruña at the beginning of the 20th century, who gradually displaced the influence of the clergy and other more conservative sectors of society.

Light and Vegetation
Modernism in A Coruña acquired a taste for ornamentation inspired on plant motifs and the use of glass which allowed the inappreciable Atlantic light into the houses.

main today as archaeological vestiges. Notes of ancient geographers and Irish legends refer to the existence of a settlement, which many affirm to have been a Phoenician colony, as part of their Tin Route. What is certain is the influence of the Romans, who are said to have built the famous lighthouse, one of the city's most emblematic monuments, in the second century. The Greek astronomer and geographer Ptolemy refers to the city as *Flavium Brigantium*, although it was later referred to as *da Farum* or *Farum Brigantium* in many historical documents and in 8th –century navigation charts. The Latin term *Crunia* appears for the first time around 1140, in the *Códice Calixtino*. By that time, many waves had beaten against its shores and its inhabitants had suffered many vicissitudes.

The Terror of the Northmen
In the 9th century, raids by the Northmen made the inhabitants of *Crunia* go inland to *La Puebla del Burgo*. The first one occurred in 844, during which the city was sacked and great damage was caused to its population. It was the first stage of a campaign that took them down the coast as far as Seville, where they were finally defeated by the troops of Abd Al-Rahman II. However, the Northmen continued attacking the coast of Galicia for more than a century.

The most important event happened in 975 when Bishop Rosendo, at the time governor of Galicia by the grace of Sancho I "El Craso" of León, gathered an army that managed to prevent an important landing of the Northmen. This action was particularly relevant since the Moors, led by Al-Hakam II, had intended to use the attack by these pirates to invade the kingdom of León. But this did not occur. Although, at the end of the tenth century, Al-Mansur reached the Atlantic coast and sacked the city of A Coruña, two centuries later the bravery of Bishop Rosendo was compensated by his being beatified.

Once the threat of the Moors was over and the city had been rebuilt, Fernando II of León used the current name of the city for the first time in 1180,

Night Universe
A panoramic view of the city lights seen from *Monte de San Pedro*.

The City's Embrace
The city seems to open up its arms and reach out to the calm waters like a friendly and welcoming gesture to those arriving at its harbour.

Gardens of Méndez Núñez
Beside the harbour and near the *Cantones*, these gardens are one of the most beautiful public spaces in A Coruña. Amidst palm trees and flower beds, one can forget about the hustle and bustle of the city.

Gardens of San Carlos
The ancient bastion of *San Carlos* was turned into gardens where, amidst trees, plants and flowers, lie the mortal remains of the British General Sir John Moore.

mentioning the *Concello de Crunia* and granting it certain autonomy. But then came the turn of the archbishops of Santiago and the Knight Templars for trying to take control of A Coruña. For some time, there was constant tension due to this motive, but, in 1208, Alfonso IX of León managed to remove "that place called Crunia, beside the lighthouse tower" from the ambitions of the nobles and turned it into an important royal enclave.

The Gateway to the Atlantic

Since the days when the Phoenicians discovered a magnificent port in the sheltered estuary, A Coruña became consolidated as such on the Atlantic coast. This is why the Romans, during the reign of Trajan, reconstructed the famous tower that, according to Celtic legend, had been built by the Celtic chieftain Breogan to guide passing boats. Even Julius Caesar had used the port of *Brigantium* when coming from *Gallia* to re-establish Roman power in that region of *Hispania*.

Due to the strategic location of the city on the Atlantic coast and its economic development, its inhabitants always defended their autonomy regarding lordly power, supporting the Crown and forming part of the seafaring brotherhood of the ports along the Cantabrian coast. Although they already held a *carta puebla* since the reign of Alfonso IX of León, the inhabitants of the city asked the Catholic Monarchs for their express promise that their city would always be connected to royal power.

However, though Carlos I chose this city as the place of Court in 1520 before leaving for Aachen (Aix-la-Chapelle) to be crowned emperor under the name of Carlos V, A Coruña was

not granted all the privileges that might have been expected.

María Pita and Sir Francis Drake

The tensions between the Spanish and British empires in the second half of the 16th century increased the strategical importance of the port of A Coruña. It was from this harbour, in 1588, that the fleet of the *Armada Invencible* left and never returned. After the naval disaster, and Felipe II's empire almost defenceless, English corsairs headed for Spanish ports. The most famous and dreaded of all, Francis Drake, attacked A Coruña on 4th May, 1589.

The corsairs, many in number, managed to break through the defences and enter the city. They got as far as the *Pescadería* and one of them was about to put up a flag as a sign of victory when a woman, standing before the body of her dead husband, took hold of his sword or spear, attacking and killing the standard bearer. This made the rest of the inhabitants react immediately against the invaders and they managed to drive them back once more.

Even though Drake's men destroyed the city, they did not succeed in conquering it. María Maior Fernández da Cámara e Pita, who has passed into history as María Pita, was the heroine of the defence of A Coruña. Her exploit did not only encourage disheartened men to fight, but also led the women of the city to take an active part in the city's defence. Another brave woman was Inés de Ben, left almost blind after being struck in the face and who, years later, was seen wandering the streets of the city she had helped to save. María Pita was more fortunate, being granted a life pension equivalent to the salary of a second lieutenant and is still homaged every August in the festivities which take place in the arcaded square where the City Hall is located and which was named after her. During these festivities the entire city is decked out and bullfights, concerts, a regatta and the reconstruction of the historical battle are all held.

The Festivity of the Senses

The historical vicissitudes of A Coruña, fully identified with those of all Galicia, have evidently fomented the religious,

The city paid homage to this famous Galician poetess who lived in A Coruña by naming this theatre after her.

Keeping Fit

One of the most popular pastimes of the locals is that of strolling through the city's pretty and quiet streets such as *La Franja* until they come across a nice place where they can enjoy a few *tapas* (savoury tidbits). In any case, a stroll through A Coruña is, for many, one of their most pleasurable everyday experiences.

merry, festive and sensual character of its inhabitants.

With the same devotion shown at the festivities in honour of the city patroness, *Nuestra Señora del Rosario*, every 7th October, and going on a pilgrimage to celebrate the *Virgen Pastoriza*, people from A Coruña open up their hearts to sensual pleasures.

In this city, called the "city of glass" by the famous writer Gonzalo Torrente Ballester, seafaring and open to the horizon of the ocean, *Albariño* and *Ribeiro* wines seem to flow as easily as the wet Atlantic winds, as well as *orujo* (marc). The latter is used to make *queimadas*, which fortify the spirit whenever necessary. However, when it comes to food, the people of this city really know what good food is.

A Coruña, being as it is a port, has always had a rich cuisine based on seafood. Some gastronomists claim that the famous *caldeirada de pescado* (fish stew) was invented by fishermen from this city. They would prepare it in their boats out at sea and, probably, some fisherman left on shore decided to set up an inn beside the harbour, and made the stew, much to the delight of the landlubbers. Álvaro Cunqueiro states in one of his numerous gastronomical essays, that *caldeirada*, maybe for being so succulent, became more popular than fish soup, which is not considered a typical dish of A Coruña cuisine. *Caldeiradas* are stews made with different kinds of fish, such as ray, angler, whose head gives the stew that special taste, mullet, conger, cod, etc., cooked with potatoes, tomatoes, green peppers and plenty oil and paprika. The typical *merluza a la gallega* is another typical dish of A Coruña, and is

a stew made with sliced hake which is baked in earthenware dishes in the oven.

Apart from the renowned shellfish (goose barnacles, lobster, spider crabs, oysters, crabs, etc.), another delicious speciality are *empanadas* (pies), the most typical one of this city being *empanada de lamprea* (lamprey eel pie). According to Galicians, the lamprey eel has aphrodisiac properties and are probably at their best in March, if we go by the saying "in March for the master and in April for the servant". Some even claim that the special properties attributed to the eels is found in their dark blood, which, if eaten in sauce, has almost immediate effects! Amongst the most learned Galicians there are many stories about erotic exploits, some of which have led their protagonists to their ruin. This is what is said to have happened to Richard the Lion Heart, who become fond of eels due to the influence of Eleanor of Aquitaine. Once he had sampled them, it is said that he liked the taste so much that he tried to eat eel every day, always being over-

In the many bars along *calle Galera* the locals enjoy tasty nibbles known as *tapas* and fine wines such as the *acidillos* from the Ulla Valley, in a scenario imbued with the aroma of legs of ham.

Chatting and Nibbling
The open-air cafés abounding in the *Plaza María Pita* are the meeting place for both locals and visitors to the capital of Galicia. Under the soft Atlantic light, the ambience of this area is filled with endless hours of friendly chatter and tapa sampling, one of the Galicians favourite pastimes.

come by its overwhelming erotic effects. This turned out to be a problem to him, especially when on crusade in the Holy Land, and it is said that when this feeling came over him, he would kneel before a church door and ask for divine pardon. Meanwhile, back in his kingdom, where his throne had been usurped by his brother John, nobody, not even Robin Hood, would eat eels.

Apart from fish and shellfish, looking inland now, Galicia is also famous for its potatoes, a crop which was brought back from the New World. Once acclimatised to Galician soil, and known as *cach-elos*, they were boiled in salted water, and superb stews together with cabbage, tomatoes, onions, ham, *chorizo*, lard, oil, garlic and, of course, paprika, were invented.

The Open City
The fact of being a port for so long has given the A Coruña an

open character, which we can see in the characteristic galleries of windows on the houses. It is rightly stated that nobody ever feels a stranger in this city due to the hospitable, fun-loving nature of its inhabitants. The urban landscape reflects this spirit, the same as its excellent wines and cuisine characterised by simple products from the land and sea. Emilia Pardo Bazán, the authoress of the well-known novel *Los pazos de Ulloa*, was born in this city and, with great realism, knew how to reflect the character of the people of this land through the struggles between peasants and nobles. Whoever comes to the city of A Coruña will be able to lean over the balcony overlooking the Atlantic Ocean and perceive, in the coming and going of the waves, the distant sound of voices coming from other peoples far beyond the horizon.

The Old Town

Colegiata de Santa María del Campo. Finished in the early 14th century, this collegiate church is a fine example of Galician Romanesque and an emblematic building of the old quarters. On the splendid tympanum of the main doorway, we can see an "Adoration of the Magi" below which many inhabitants of the city meet on summer evenings, just like in the past.

The Old Town

Romanesque Splendour. The interior of the *Colegiata de Santa María* del Campo with its sturdy columns and Romanesque-style ribbed arches creates an atmosphere which invites us to pray, envelopped by a light that seems an ethereal mark of the souls belonging to medieval priests and nobles whose tombs are preserved here.

Bell Tower. Stone and bell, silence and noise, are perhaps the basic elements of a spiritual metaphor that the ancient Galicians expressed through the creation of the *Colegiata de Santa María del Campo*.

The Stone Cruceiro (Cross) in front of the *Colegiata de Santa María del Campo* indicates the site of a Christian church.

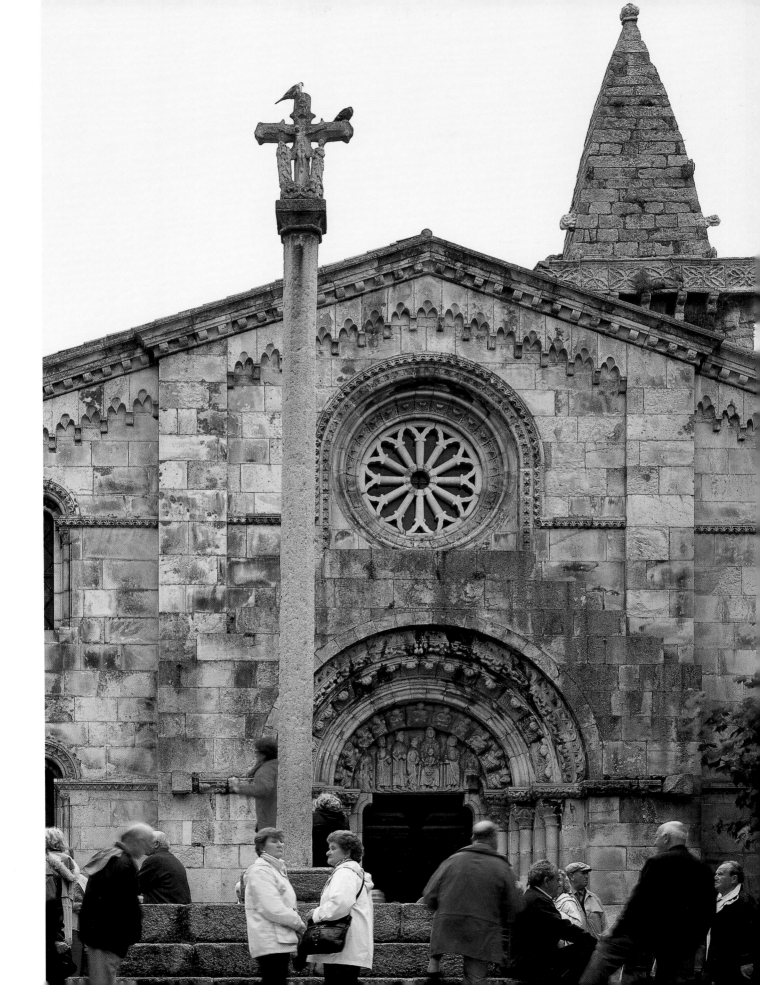

Church of Santo Domingo. The magnificent bell tower of this 18th –century Baroque church houses bells that ring out over the whole city as reminders of prayer and Mass.

Light and Shade. The narrow streets of the old town, such as *Puerta de Aires*, seem to be painting chiaroscuros left by history over the centuries.

Christian Faith. In the small, peaceful *Plaza de las Bárbaras*, a cross and an allegorical relief of Saint Michael weighing souls on the stone façade of the 15th –century Convent of *Las Clarisas*.

The Old Town

Coat of Arms. Just one of the numerous coats of arms that can be seen on the façades of mansions standing along the narrow streets of the old town, a living example of Galician history.

Church of Santiago. The oldest Christian church in the city where beautiful mouldings and sculptures adorn the main portal, one of the best examples of Galician Romanesque art.

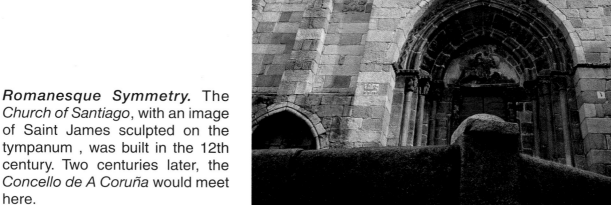

Romanesque Symmetry. The *Church of Santiago*, with an image of Saint James sculpted on the tympanum , was built in the 12th century. Two centuries later, the *Concello de A Coruña* would meet here.

The Old Town

The Circle Beneath the Cross.
Finely-adorned rose window
through which the light enters the
Church of Santiago.

The Curve in the Stone. The audacity of the ribbed arches of the Romanesque *Church of Santiago* is just like that of the city's inhabitants who used one of its towers as a magazine during the 16th century.

The Lamb of God. The image of the nun at the window on the western side of the *Church of Santiago* is in tone with the Christian symbology carved in stone and in keeping with the ancient Romanesque architecture.

The Old Town

The New Town

Dársena de la Marina. Whilst the old part of the town was built on the peninsula, the new part extends from the isthmus inland. This is the sector popularly known as *La Pescadería* ("The Fishmonger's") as it was where fishermen and merchants concentrated their products. Here, in the shelter of the harbour, and along the seafront, we can see the typical houses with their glass galleries and balconies.

The Light of Modernism. In 1833, the Council of A Coruña carried out important reforms through the new Development Plan. The area known as *La Pescadería*, where the local middle-class merchants who had become wealthy thanks to overseas trade built their Modernist-style houses, whose façades were adorned with plant motifs.

The New Town

Galleries on the Seafront. The Modernist glass façades, designed to make the most of the light and protect the houses from the Atlantic winds, gave the new part a distinguished character which, from that moment was called the "city of glass".

Casa del Rey. Overlooking the *Plaza de María*, we have this Modernist monument with its wavy-shaped cornice, glazed ceramics, wrought-iron balconies and elegant lines of its glass gallery.

Congress Hall and Auditorium. In the heart of the city, on the former site of a quarry, we can find this modern, classic-style building featuring splendid columns.

Church of San Jorge. This 18th—century Baroque church on the edge of the old town has magnificent sculptures and has been declared an Historic-Artistic Monument.

The New Town

The New Town

Palacio Municipal. Early twentieth-century Modernist building whose solid structure is, to the people of A Coruña, an expression of the deep roots of civil power as a symbol of government.

In Memory of the Heroes. Traditions are important to the inhabitants of A Coruña, who hold great respect for those who gave their lives for the city, as we can see from this monument to Curros Enríquez, by the sculptor Asorey.

The New Town

Noble Floor. The layout and décor of the interior of the *Palacio Municipal* recreate an atmosphere of rigour in accordance with the principles of civil power and authority.

The New Town

Plaza del Humor. With the Market of *San Agustín* in the background, this square has been dedicated to fine Galician humorists such as Cunquiero and Castelao.

Market of San Agustín. This building with its glass vaults has been renovated like a modern cathedral to food.

Quiosco Alfonso. An interesting building which is a place of important exhibitions in the Gardens of *Méndez Núñez*.

The New Town

Modernist News-stand. We can buy newspapers and magazines at this quaint kiosk located on *Calle del Riego de Agua*.

The Power of the New Sector. The *Avenida de La Marina* and the *Calle Cantón Grande* with its popular obelisk, mark a neuralgic point of modern A Coruña.

The New Town

Traffic and Business. In the heart of the district known as *La Pescadería* a publicity sign amidst tall glass buildings is a natural component of the urban landscape.

The Direction of Time. The Obelisk dedicated to Aureliano Linares Rivas is crowned by a weather vane and a clock with four spheres which seem to point out the mysterious direction of time to the inhabitants of A Coruña.

Squares, Gardens and Museums

The Heart of A Coruña. The *Plaza de María Pita* is the public space that marks the historic frontier between the old town and the new sector of the city which is characterised by its beautiful glass galleries; a neuralgic point of the city where we can see the statue of the local heroine in the square named after her. Also to be highlighted is the *Palacio Municipal*, this temple of sovereignty is where local affairs are debated and regulated.

Plaza de María Pita. The arcades hardly alter the geometric lines of the urban landscape designed for a city characterised by its strong will and determination. A favourite place for taking a leisurely stroll.

Squares, Gardens and Museums

Day and Night in the *Plaza de María Pita* are like seasons of a constant dream of the future rooted in the deepest traditions of Galicians.

Plaza General de Azcárraga. Square dedicated to the soldier who fought to get A Coruña granted its own military headquarters, the building being near the former 18th -century *Real Audiencia*.

Square of the Past. What is known today as the *Plaza General de Azcárraga* used to be part of the former *Plaza de la Harina* or *Fariña* where public executions would take place.

Plazuela de las Bárbaras or ***de Santa Bárbara***. Built on the site of an ancient hermitage dedicated to this saint, in the heart of the city, today it houses the old Convent of *Las Clarisas*, in front of which we can see a typical *cruceiro* (cross).

Squares, Gardens and Museums

Plaza de la Constitución. Taking up part of the old *Plaza de la Fariña*, where the impressive building of the *Church of Santiago* stands, featuring solid stonework and the typical Romanesque architecture which prevailed in Galicia between the 12th and 15th centuries.

Cruceiro de la Constitución. This typical monument of Christ on the Cross reminds us of the historical connection between Galicia and the spirit of Christendom, in the heart of the city.

Church of Santiago. The head and transept of the church mark one of the sides of the *Plaza de la Constitución*, haunted, according to the superstitious, by the souls of those who were executed.

Squares, Gardens and Museums

Rosaleda Park. A broad, lush prolongation of the *Gardens of Méndez Núñez* situated near the streets of *Los Cantones*, marks a neuralgic point of the new town where there is a high concentration of shops and open-air cafés.

Island of Peace. *La Rosaleda* is a haven of peace amidst the bustling area of *La Pescadería*, where windows are known as "consolations" due to their soothing effect.

Squares, Gardens

and Museums

Plazuela de Santo Domingo. With its small, simple fountain and its façades featuring beautiful windows and wrought-iron balconies, we feel as if we are in the Garden of Earthly Delights, where many come to read amidst the peace and tranquillity.

Squares, Gardens and Museums

Plaza de Portugal. Overlooking the sea, with its flowerbeds and fountains with sculptures of seagulls in flight, this square is a metaphor of the modern city that looks to the future.

Aquarium. Like a mysterious tunnel taking us into the deep sea world, we are led into the modern aquarium of A Coruña where we can wonder at a wide range of different shapes and colours of sea creatures and plants.

Gabinete del Capitán Nemo. Maybe Jules Verne's famous character could admire the same marvels of the sea from his submarine, *Nautilus*.

Ocean Riches. The *Casa de los Peces* ("House of the Fish"), as the aquarium is also known, shows us the secrets of the sea directly and through interactive displays.

Squares,
Gardens
and Museums

Museum of Clocks. Perhaps it is due to the peculiar notion of time held by the inhabitants of this city that a section of the City Council was reformed to house a splendid collection of clocks.

Squares, Gardens and Museums

Archaeological Museum. Located in the Castle of *San Antón*, this museum belonging to the A Coruña City Council houses valuable pieces of primitive local pottery and items telling us of ancient Celtic settlements.

Historical Treasures. Primitive sculptures form part of the collection of a museum which lets us discover distant aspects of everyday life and culture in these northern lands of the Peninsula.

Squares, Gardens and Museums

The Museum of Mankind (Domus). A sail in the wind, a flexible, resistant, driving element, is the architectonic metaphor of the building that houses the museum dedicated to the human being as an individual and as a species.

To Be or Not to Be. The fragile bony structure of a pensive figure evokes to us the passing of time and the fugacity of the flesh. The awareness of life and death are synthesised in this well-known sentence placed by Shakespeare in the mouth of Hamlet.

The Double Spiral of DNA. Only with the knowledge gathered over centuries has Man been able to build the genetic pattern of human life, the basic code that explains the organic existence of mankind.

The House of Science. Established in 1983, this was the first public interactive centre of scientific and technological divulgation created in Spain for people of all ages.

Technological Forms. Popular and industrial mechanics have a significant space in the so-called House of Science, where the public can learn by enjoying themselves through active participation.

House-Museum of Emilia Pardo Bazán. Formerly the home of the famous authoress of *Los Pazos de Ulloa*, today the building still contains many of her belongings and is the Royal Academy Of Galician Arts and Letters.

Museum of Fine Arts. Standing on the site of an old convent of Capuchin nuns, this museum houses magnificent collections of Flemish, Italian, Spanish and, above all, Galician paintings.

Squares, Gardens and Museums

From the Tower of Hercules

Lighthouse of the Atlantic. Legend has it that the tower was built in the days of the Celtic chieftain Breogan to commemorate the departure of an expedition to Ireland. Historians claim that it was in the 2nd century, during the reign of the Roman emperor Trajan, when this square lighthouse was erected, which has been working since then, warning sailors of the proximity of the coast.

From the Tower of Hercules

Inside the Tower. The oldest working lighthouse in Europe, whose construction has been attributed by some to Hercules and by others to the Celtic chieftain Breogan, used to have a steep ramp inside. However, the latter was replaced in 1791 by an imposing spiral staircase consisting of 242 steps.

Symbol of A Coruña. The three-bodied, square tower-lighthouse, measure 64 metres high and was reformed at the end of the 18th century.

The Eyes of the Lighthouse. From the top of the tower, our eye scans the beach and retains the image of the sea foam on the *Gran Caracola*.

Ancient Rites. These prehistoric lithic monuments, common to the primitive settlers of Galicia, can be seen in the "Field of Menhirs" located in the Tower of Hercules Park. The Greek geographer Strabo was the first to mention them, basing himself on writings of others, for example, Artemidoros who visited *Hispania* around 100 BC.

From the Tower of Hercules

From the Tower of Hercules

Watch Tower. It is also said that the name of the city comes from the Celtic term, *coryn*, meaning "strip of land". And, at the end of this strip, stands the tower that watches over the heavy sea traffic coming to A Coruña Port.

Moored Boats. In the Atlantic light, the small, empty, boats look as if they were strange, motionless water flowers, perhaps a rare species of water lily awaiting the impulse of the current.

From the Tower of Hercules

The Wide Ria. From the Promenade, a passer-by looks over the calm waters of the A Coruña ria, on whose left bank the city was built.

On Track. The old tramway, which follows the shore of the ria, gives the city a certain personality, connecting historical places between the Castle of *San Antón* and the Tower of Hercules.

La Maestranza Gardens. Next to the calm waters of the ria, open spaces provide a touch of colour and open air to the old part of the city full of narrow medieval streets.

Paseo Marítimo. In spite of being a harbour, A Coruña has always lived with its back to the sea until 1986 when this promenade was built along the shore, thus changing its inhabitants' age-old customs, who now come here to stroll.

Castle of San Antón. When Carlos I decided to establish the *Casa de Contratación de Especias* (The Spice Exchange) in A Coruña it was necessary to build a fortress to defend the city from pirate attacks. This was the origin of this castle, built with stones from the old walls on an islet at the mouth of the ria, and which today is the Archaeological Museum.

From the Tower of Hercules

Silhouette. The layout of the Castle of *San Antón*, with its irregular angles and its sloping, battlemented walls and towers, makes it look as if it were a natural part of the islet. *(Next two pages.)*

Riazor and Orzán Beaches

Caressed by the Waves. From the Promenade, we can see the beaches known as Riazor and Orzán, which are also a result of the impulse and effort carried out by the people of A Coruña to make the most of their proximity to the sea. When the weather is fine visitors and locals flock here to sunbathe, to swim or to do a bit of surfing and this is where bonfires are lit on the Midsummer Night.

Riazor and Orzán Beaches

Monument to Surfers. A festive tribute to those who surf the huge waves at Orzán Bay.

Night View. When darkness falls, the beach seems to softly surrender to the sound of the waves.

Riazor and Orzán Beaches. The jetty marks the limit between the two beaches frequented by those who come here for sheer pleasure.

Riazor and Orzán Beaches

Orzán Bay. Cirrus clouds look like an extension of the ripples on the surface of the waters caressing the shores of the inlet, whose extremes appear lit up by the night lights of a city that is ready for sleep.

Urban Crest. From the top of a building we have a fine view of Orzán Bay and the city rooftops.

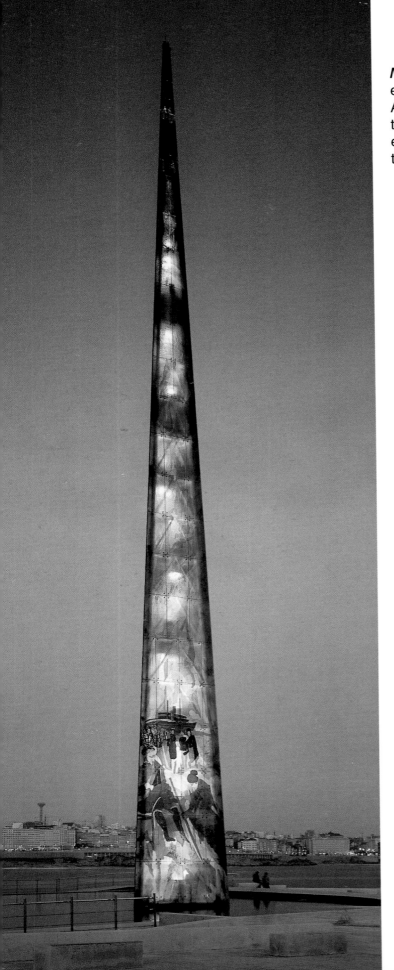

Millennium. The name of this superb monument erected at one end of the *Paseo Marítimo*, with which A Coruña welcomed the arrival of the twenty-first century and the new millennium. Since then, it is lit up every night like a ray of history directed at the future, towards which A Coruña is looking.

Riazor and Orzán Beaches

Monument to Hope. The Millennium monument, in the district of *Labañou*, is a 50-metre steel obelisk, adorned with rock crystal representing scenes of historical events occurring in the city. It is surrounded by a pond into which people throw coins, making a wish as they do so.

Twilight. Clouds build up as darkness falls over the city, whose buildings are terraced out toward the sea as the street lights and the obelisk come alight. *(Next two pages.)*

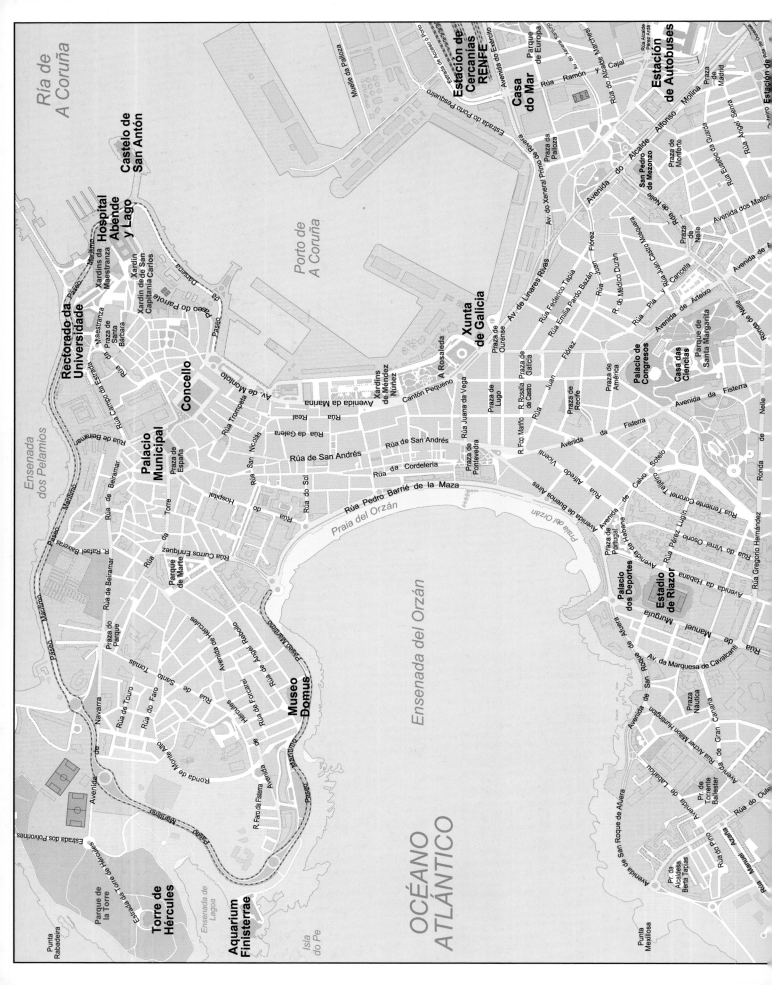